THE OPEN TUNING CHORD BOOK FOR GUITAR

Published by
Wise Publications

Exclusive Distributor for the United States, Canada,
Mexico and U.S. possessions:

Order No. AM1001825
ISBN 978-0-8256-3759-9
HL Item Number: 14037770

Edited by Tom Farncombe.
Original design and layout by Stuart Eadie.
Back cover photo by Jo Erskine.

Printed in the United States of America

 HAL•LEONARD®

Visit Hal Leonard Online at
www.halleonard.com

ct us:
onard
emound Road
WI 53213
lleonard.com

contact:
urope Limited
42 Wigmore Street
Marylebone, London, W1U 2RN
Email: info@halleonardeurope.com

In Australia, contact:
Hal Leonard Australia Pty. Ltd.
4 Lentara Court
Cheltenham, Victoria, 3192 Australia
Email: info@halleonard.com.au

ACKNOWLEDGEMENTS

Much thanks to Stuart Coupe, Alex Smythe,
Peter Doyle, Simon Day, Paul Nearhos, Stuart Eadie
and Lee-Anne for their help on my little project.

This book is dedicated to Ry Cooder.

Brendan Gallagher has been playing guitar
for nearly 40 years. Best known as singer/songwriter
with Aussie cult band Karma County he is also
an award winning producer with over 20 albums to his
credit. His distinctive open tuned and slide guitar playing
can be heard on recordings by artists like
David Bowie, Jimmy Little and Kylie Minogue.
To find out more about Brendan and his music go to
www.brendangallagher.com.au

★

"The 'Open Tuning Chord Book for Guitar'
is a wonderful introduction to the world of
altered tunings. Different guitar tunings really
open up the textural possibilities of the guitar
and Brendan's book does a great job of presenting
these different textures in a very organized and fun way.
It's sure to breathe new life into your playing!"
LEE RITENOUR

*"I have being playing for 50 years
and there is always something new that
somebody can show me."*
ARLO GUTHRIE

"Inspiring... Brendan Gallagher's 'Open Tuning
Chord Book For Guitar' will introduce guitarists to
a whole new palette of sounds. An essential
companion for anyone interested in exploring
the possibilities of the guitar."
**AMANDA BROWN
(THE GO-BETWEENS)**

*"Releases the shackles of standard tuning
and it's obvious from the first page that it has been
written by someone who really plays."*
MARK LIZOTTE A.K.A. DIESEL

"Either he or I better have good lawyers
'cause I'm gonna steal every f***in' thing he's got!"
TIM ROGERS (YOU AM I)

*"Buy two copies – because one is sure to be
stolen by anyone you show it to"*
**GENEVIEVE MAYNARD
(STELLA ONE ELEVEN)**

"Brendan's book is a playground for my fingers
and my ears. I can find where all those 'other' chords
are hiding – in minutes instead of years –
and still play amongst the luscious open tunings
and resonating strings that make me happy.
Thank you Brendan, 'The Open Tuning Chord Book'
is a groundbreaking gift to us all."
JODI MARTIN

CONTENTS

★

★

Why, When, Where?

The purpose of this book is to give guitarists working in standard tuning a basic introduction into open tuned guitar playing. In open tunings it is possible to achieve unisons, colours, and chords that give a different perspective to the guitar.

Though commonly used for *slide* guitar before now, open tunings have become increasingly popular for their unusual and rich voicings. If using a slide, though, it is still possible to achieve most chords with the remaining three fingers and/or thumb.

The two tunings shown here are generally the most popular. They are: *Vastopol*, also known as *Open D*, and *Spanish*, also known as *Open G* or *Low Bass G*. In the following text I'll refer to them as Open D and Open G respectively.

The *concert* or *standard* tuning of the guitar is a relatively recent phenomenon. In the traditional music of Celtic and other European cultures, open tunings were predominant, mainly being played on the guitar's precursor, the lute. The instruments that ended up in the hands of the African-Americans in the Mississippi Delta and concurrently the indigenous people of the Hawaiian Islands, were adapted to suit the musical expression of the two respective peoples. The propensity for slide playing in the Delta (which was better facilitated with a full open chord tuning) and the disposition to a manually easier technique amongst the Hawaiians (hence the *slack key* method so named for the slackness of the de-tuned strings) led to the proliferation of Open D and Open G guitar.

The names Vastopol and Spanish are supposedly the products of a sales push by the Gibson Mandolin-Guitar Manufacturing Company in the U.S.A. at the begining of the twentieth century when the guitar was a poor cousin to the banjo and violin. A concerted effort by Gibson to sell product incorporated a sales pitch where the guitar was tuned to open D and the aspiring picker was taught 'The Seige Of Sebastopol', a parlour tune from the Crimean War period which was perfectly suited to open D. The ensuing years rounded the pronunciation and spelling off to Vastopol which subsequently became the name associated with that tuning.

Similarly the low bass G tuning became associated with the song 'Spanish Fandango' and again the amelioration of the title produced Spanish tuning.

These tunings can be seen as stepping-off points for other tunings (lute, Hawaiian sixth and major seventh, Irish etc.). The variations are limitless. Witness the palette of Curtis Mayfield, who tunes to the black keys of the piano (F$\sharp$,A$\sharp$,C$\sharp$,F$\sharp$,A$\sharp$,F$\sharp$) or Keith Richards, who often uses open G but discards the sixth string, or the late Albert Collins who worked with an open minor chord tuning capoed at the third fret.

The changing of guitar tuning may seem a dizzying experience for those grounded in standard chord shapes but it can be immensely rewarding, not only for its own sake, but as a compositional and arranging tool as well. Apply some standard tuning chord shapes to an open tuned guitar and you will find some interesting territory to explore. Experiment!

How So?

The whole basis of open tuning is, obviously, to change the tuning of the guitar from standard (**E**,**A**,**D**,**G**,**B**,**E**) to other voicings. Some care should be exercised in the process. Why?

Scenario A: inadvertantly, citizen X winds string up beyond the threshold of human hearing and...
Result: snaps and cleaves off nose.
Scenario B: citizen X attaches inordinately thick string to guitar and...
Result: ends up with neck with more bow than Robin Hood.

So, here are some helpful hints:

★ The two tunings used in this book involve *loosening* strings. In open D the 1st, 2nd, 3rd and 6th strings are de-tuned. In Open G the 1st, 5th, and 6th are de-tuned. This may produce an uncomfortable slackness or some ringing overtones when plucked (or both). Consider using a slightly heavier guage string. This should return a loosened string to the tension you are used to and hopefully eliminate any ringing.

★ If you change from a wound to an unwound string, or vice versa (usually the 3rd string), you may have to adjust the bridge intonation or the string won't tune correctly. Generally, unless it's a fixed bridge, it's not a problem. If it is, consult a guitar tech.

★ When tuning a string give it a few gentle stretches with the picking hand before winding the tuning peg. This will set the tension in the machine head a little quicker. Remember, be careful of broken strings.

★ Finally, *trust your own ears*. If it sounds right, move on.

And The Chords Are...

There are twelve chords for each key. They are as follows:

Major: A, C etc
Minor: Am, Cm etc
Sixth: A^6, C^6 etc
Dominant seventh: A^7, C^7 etc
Diminished: A^o, C^o etc
Augmented: A+ , C+ etc
Minor sixth: Am^6; Cm^6 etc
Major seventh: $Amaj^7$, $Cmaj^7$ etc
Minor seventh: Am^7, Cm^7 etc
Seventh suspended fourth: A^7sus^4, C^7sus^4 etc
Dominant seventh flat ninth: $A^{7\flat9}$, $C^{7\flat9}$ etc
Eleventh: A^{11}, C^{11} etc

Nuts And Bolts

★ The fingerings for fretting are designated as follows:
   1 = index finger
   2 = middle finger
   3 = ring finger
   4 = pinky

★ The guitar strings are numbered 1 to 6, high to low i.e., the 1st string is the highest tuned or treble string, the 6th string is the lowest tuned or bass string.

★ Alternately, the keys of the strings are referred to in ascending scale e.g., standard tuning is, low to high, **E,A,D,G,B,E**.

★ The interval between each fret is referred to as one half-tone or one half-step; the interval between two frets is called one tone or one whole step.

★ A number appearing at the top right-hand side of an individual chord chart (below) denotes a fingering position at that fret. In this case, the 1st finger barres across the third fret, the 2nd finger is on fourth fret of the 3rd string and the 3rd finger is on the fifth fret of the 4th string. Otherwise, the top line of the chord chart denotes the nut.

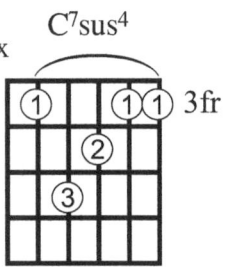

C^7sus^4

Open D Tuning

The first series of chords are for Open D. The guitar is tuned, low to high: **D**,**A**,**D**,**F**[♯],**A**,**D**. You should recognize this as a D major chord. To produce this from a standard tuned guitar, proceed as follows:

E or 6th:	tune down a whole step to		**D**
A or 5th:	remains the same		**A**
D or 4th:	remains the same		**D**
G or 3rd:	tune down a half-step to		**F**[♯]
B or 2nd:	tune down a whole step to		**A**
E or 1st:	tune down a whole step to		**D**

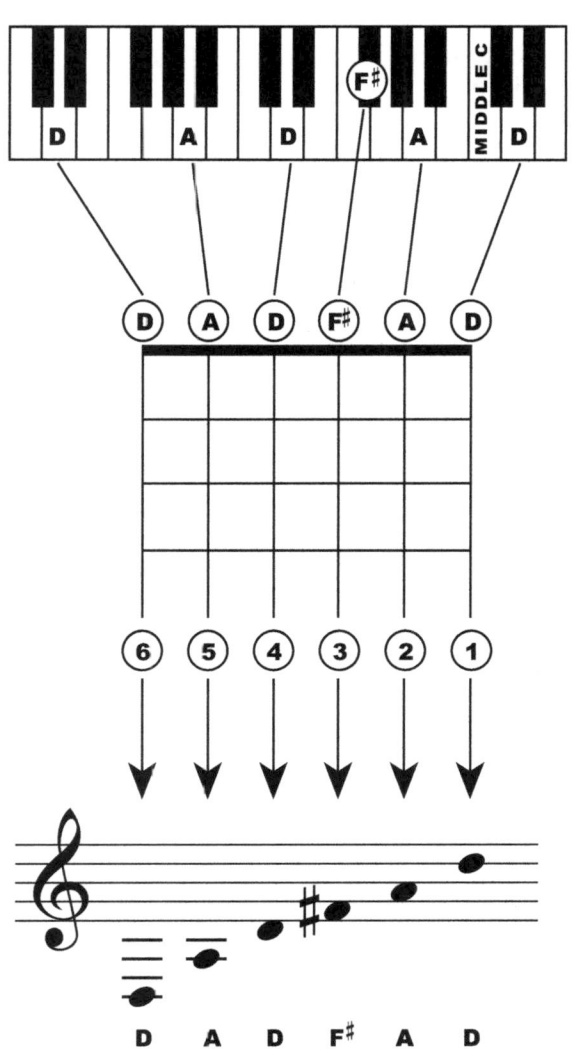

In my experience, the best way to achieve this, aside from a chromatic tuner, is to tune the guitar with a combination of harmonics and fretting.

First, tune the E or 6th string down a whole step to D using a piano, tuner, tuning fork etc. Pluck the 6th string while lightly touching it directly above the seventh fret wire, but not pressing on to the fretboard. This will produce a sustained A harmonic one octave above the open A or 5th string.

Do the same at the twelfth fret of the 5th string. This should produce the same note. If not, adjust the 5th string tuning peg until it does. The rest of the tuning should follow: the fifth fret harmonic of the 5th string should match the seventh fret harmonic of the 4th string; the seventh fret harmonic of the 4th string should match the twelfth fret harmonic of the 2nd string; the fifth fret harmonic of the 4th string should match the twelfth fret harmonic of the 1st string; fretting the 4th string at the fourth fret should match the open 3rd string.

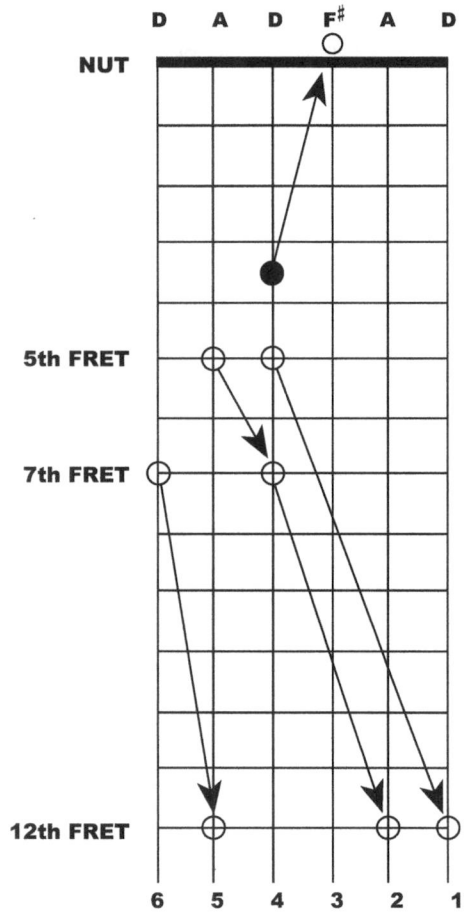

Open G Tuning

The second series of chords are for Open G. The guitar is tuned, low to high, **D,G,D,G,B,D**. To produce this from standard tuning, proceed as follows:

E or 6th:	tune down a whole step to	**D**
A or 5th:	tune down a whole step to	**G**
D or 4th:	remains the same	**D**
G or 3rd:	remains the same	**G**
B or 2nd:	remains the same	**B**
E or 1st:	tune down a whole step to	**D**

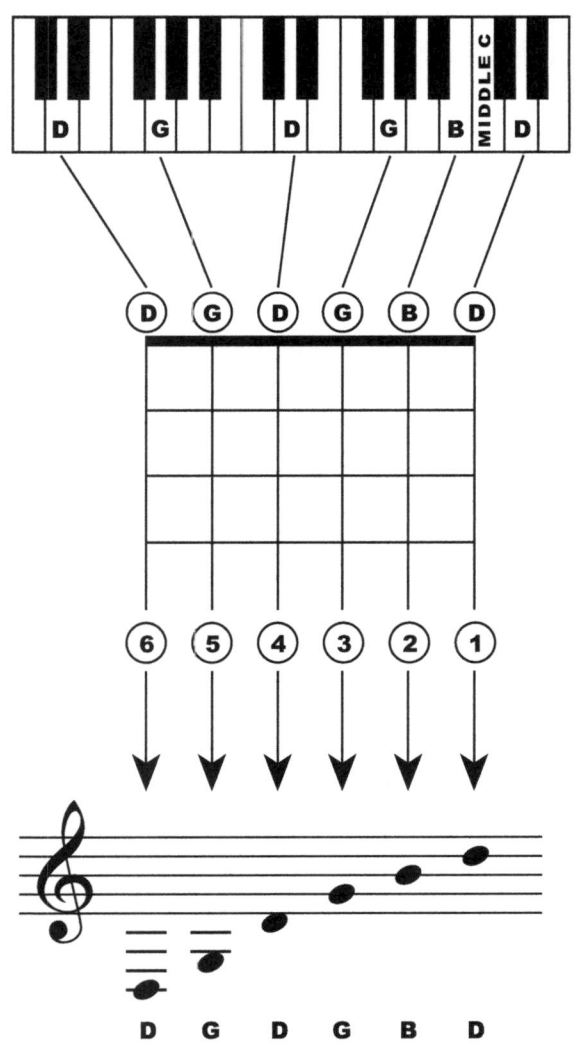

This is achieved, again, with a combination of harmonics and fretting. First, tune the sixth string down a whole step to D. The fifth fret harmonic on the 6th string should match the twelfth fret harmonic on the 4th string; the fifth fret harmonic on the 4th string should match the twelfth fret harmonic on the 1st string; fretting the 4th string at the fifth fret should match the open 3rd string; the twelfth fret harmonic on the 3rd string should match the fifth fret harmonic or the 5th string; fretting the 3rd string at the fourth fret should match the open 2nd string.

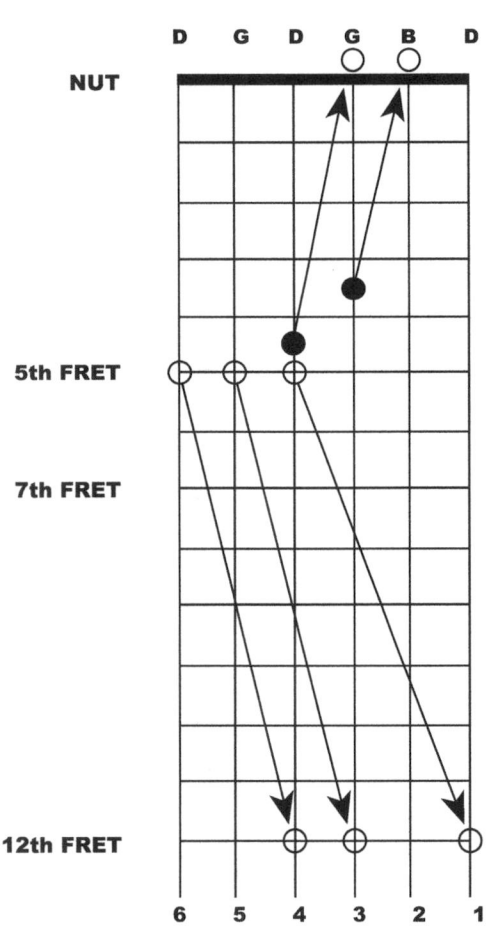

Some root position chords are difficult to fret and there are cases where a third or fifth is used as the lowest note, but remember, these chord shapes are only some of the many variations you can apply. Just as in standard tuning there is more than one way to play a chord, so it is in open tunings. It's up to you to find them on the fretboard.

Open D: root D

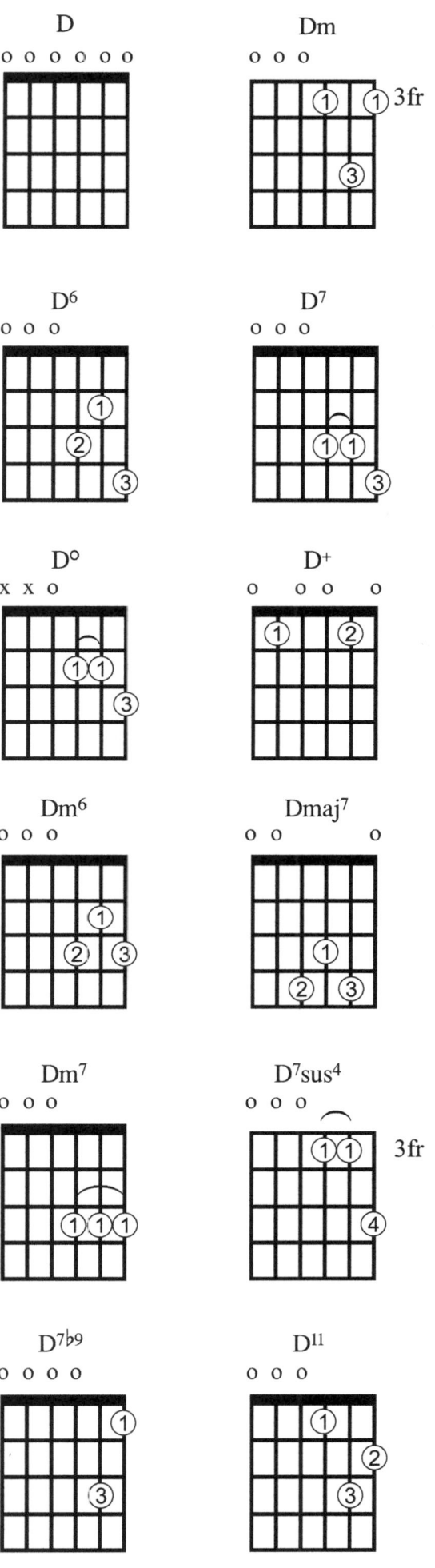

Open D: root E♭

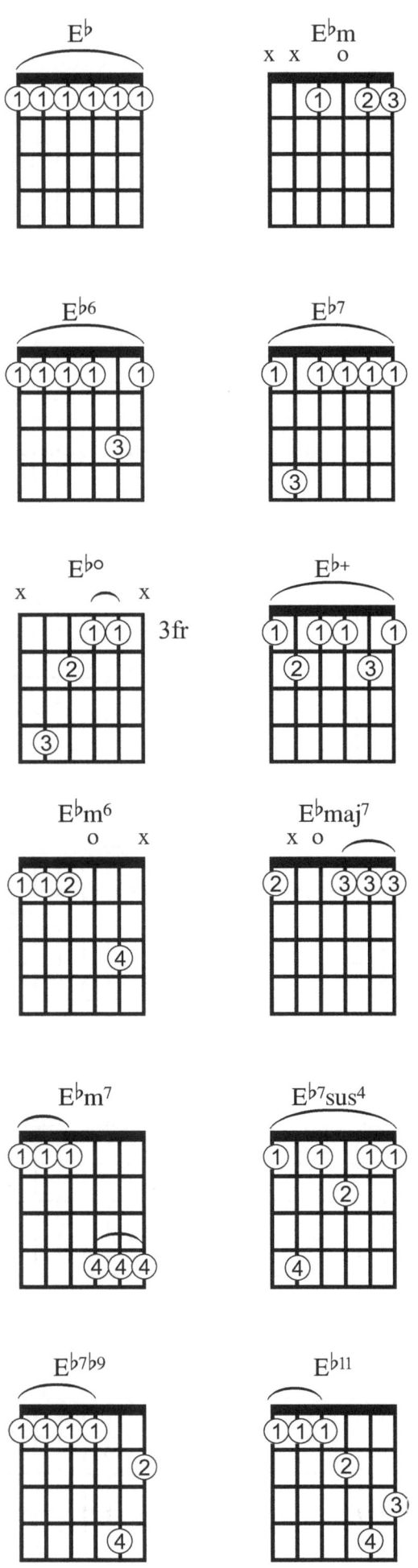

Open D: root E

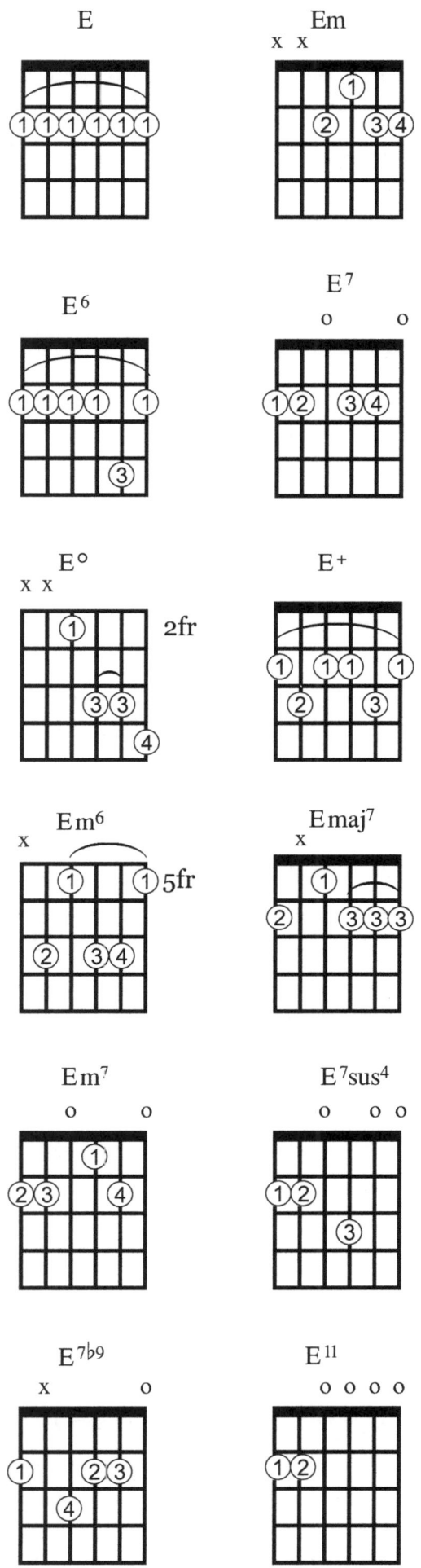

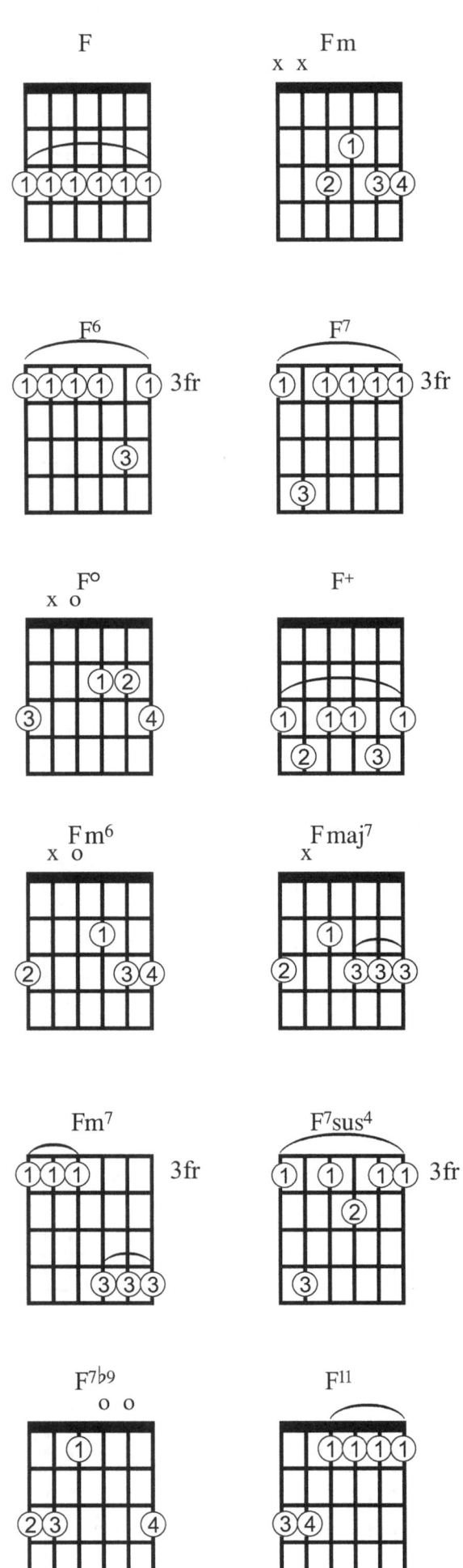

Open D: root F#

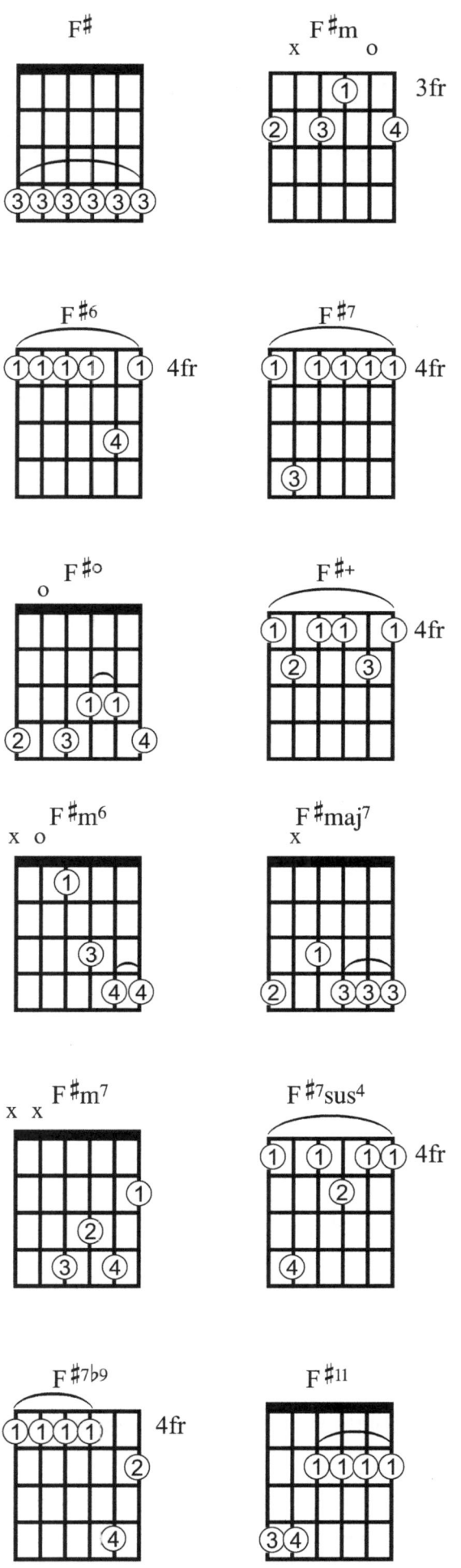

Open D: root G

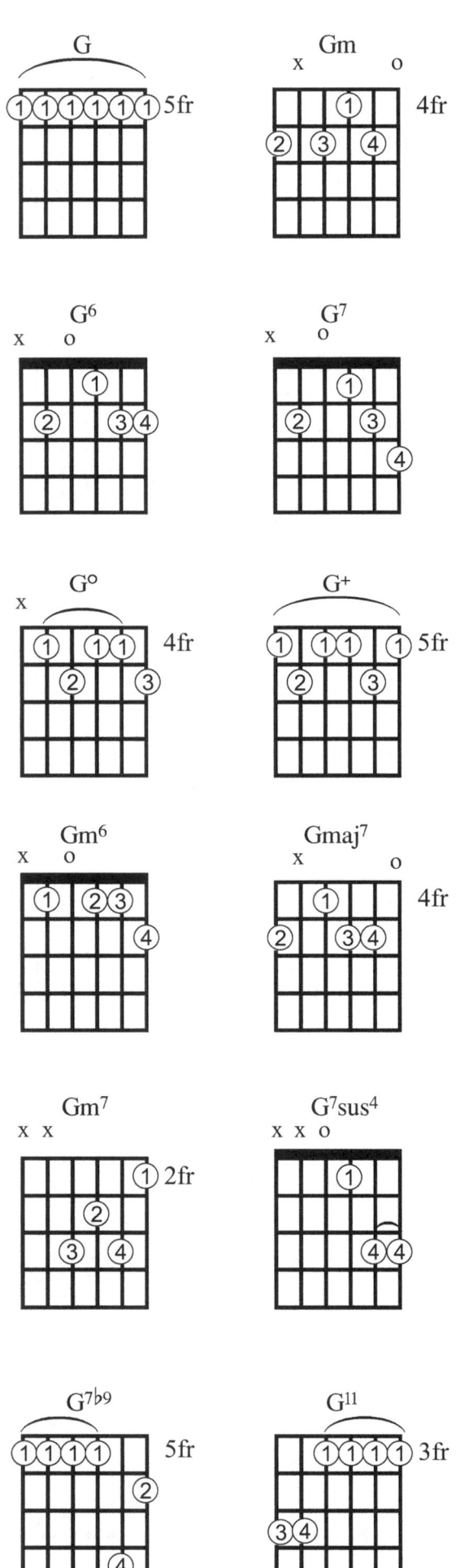

Open D: root A♭

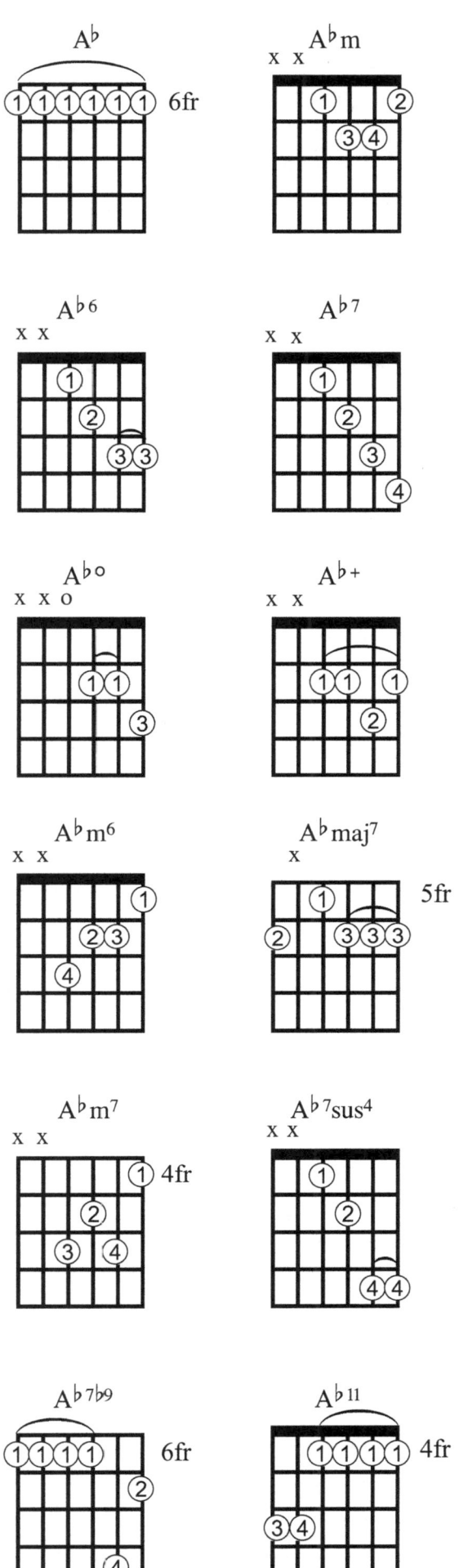

Open D: root A

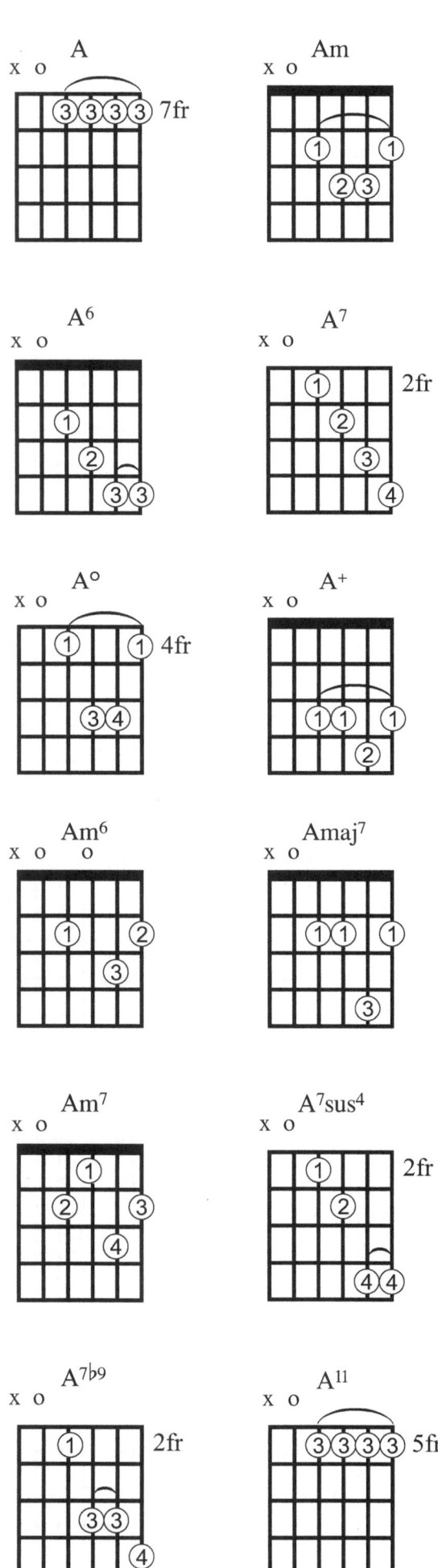

Open D: root B♭

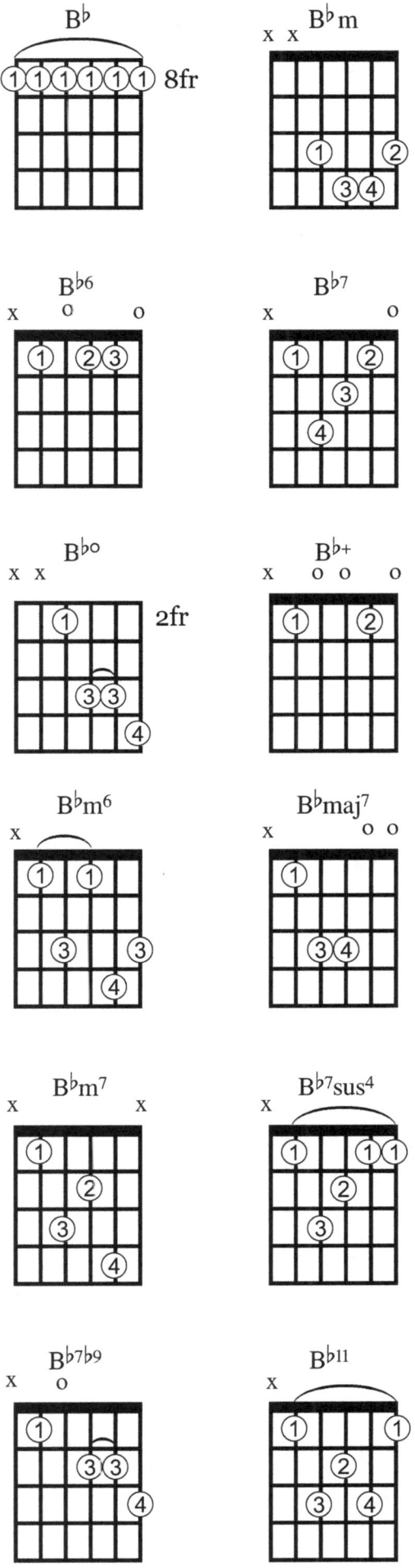

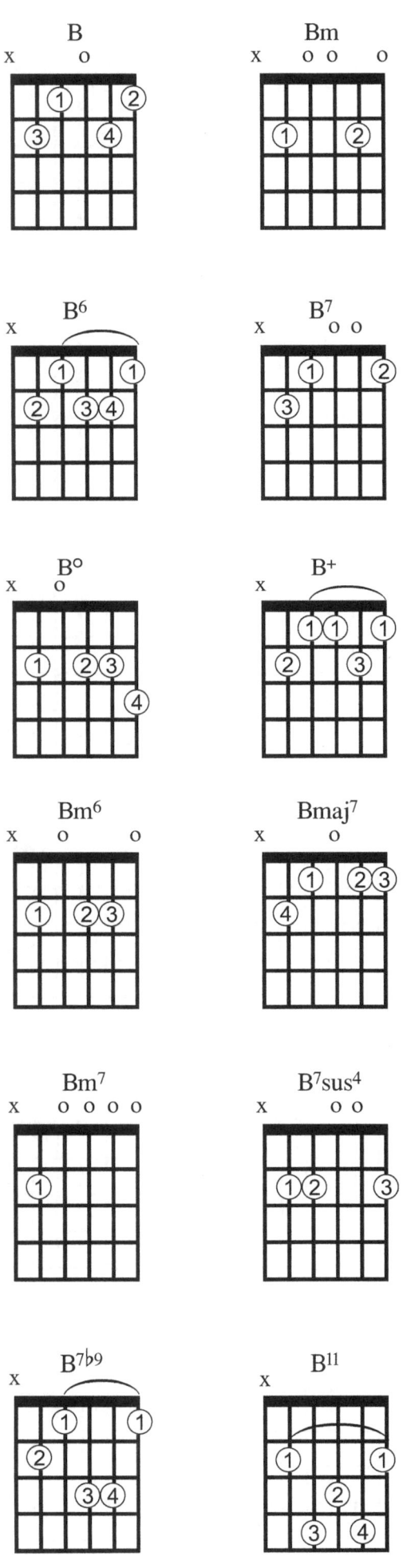

B   Bm

B^6 B^7

B$^{\circ}$ B$^+$

Bm^6 Bmaj^7

Bm^7 B^{7}sus^4

B$^{7\flat9}$ B^{11}

Open D: root C

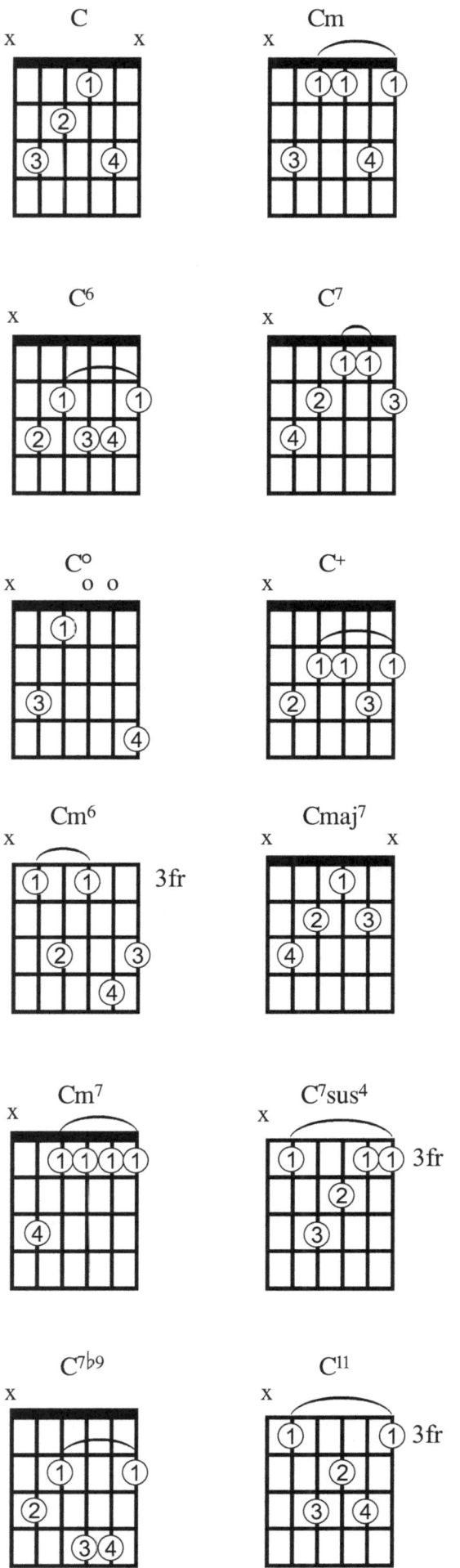

Open D: root C#

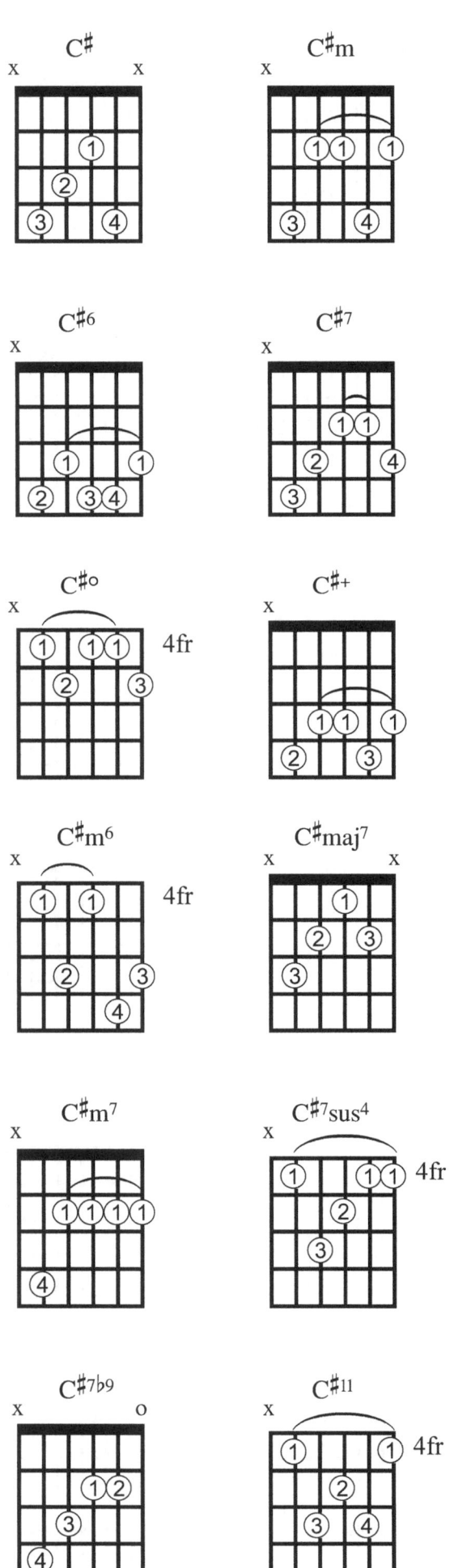

C#

C#m

C#6

C#7

C#o   4fr

C#+

C#m6   4fr

C#maj7

C#m7

C#7sus4   4fr

C#7b9

C#11   4fr

23

Favourite Open D Chords

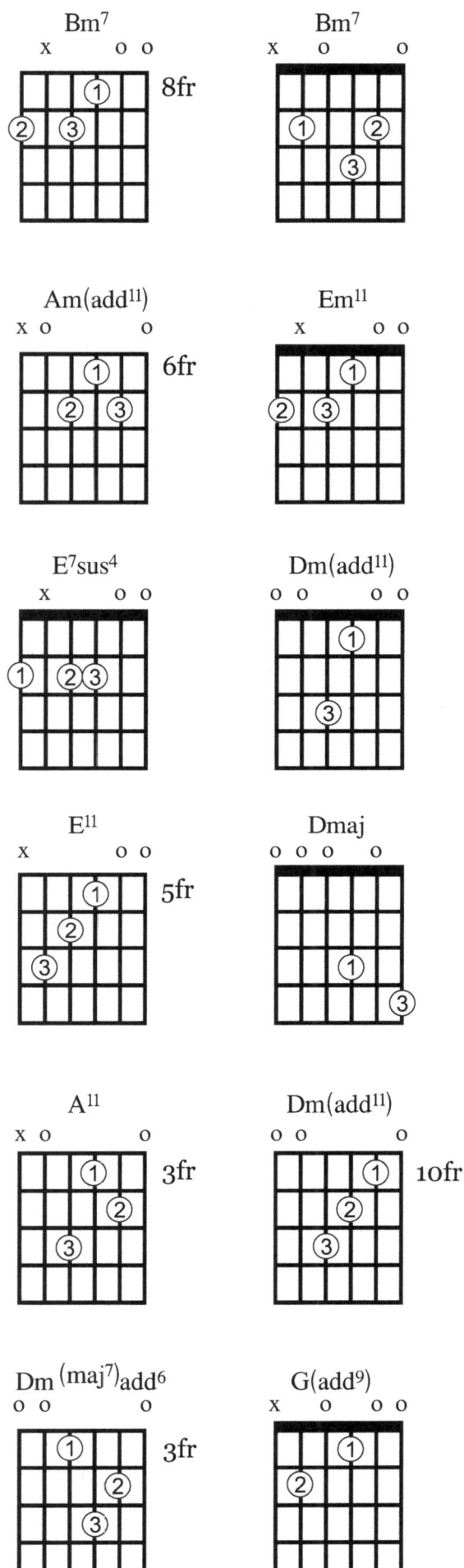

24

Open G: root G

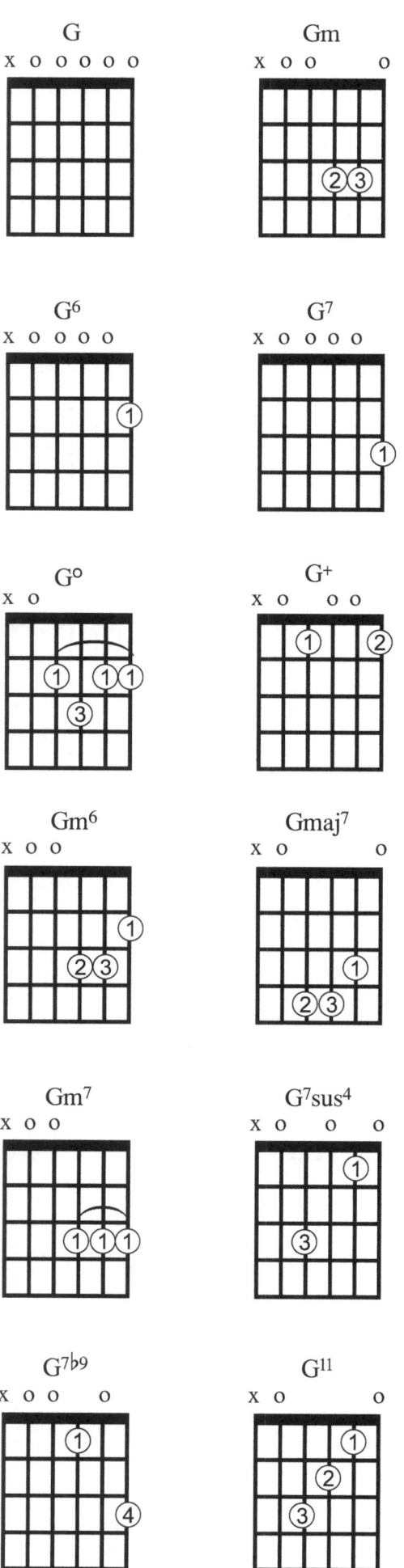

Open G: root A♭

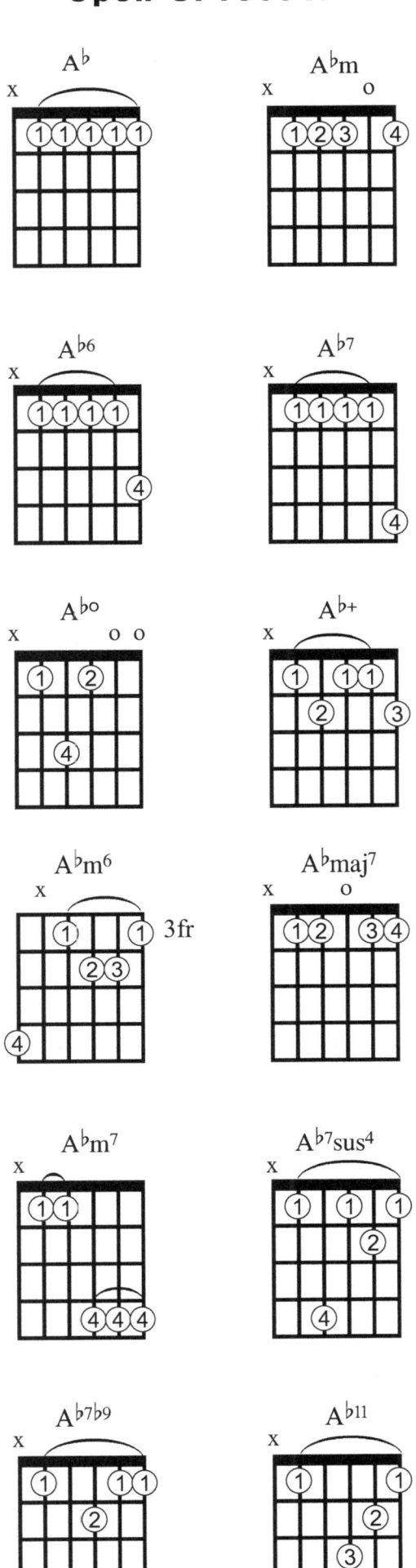

Open G: root A

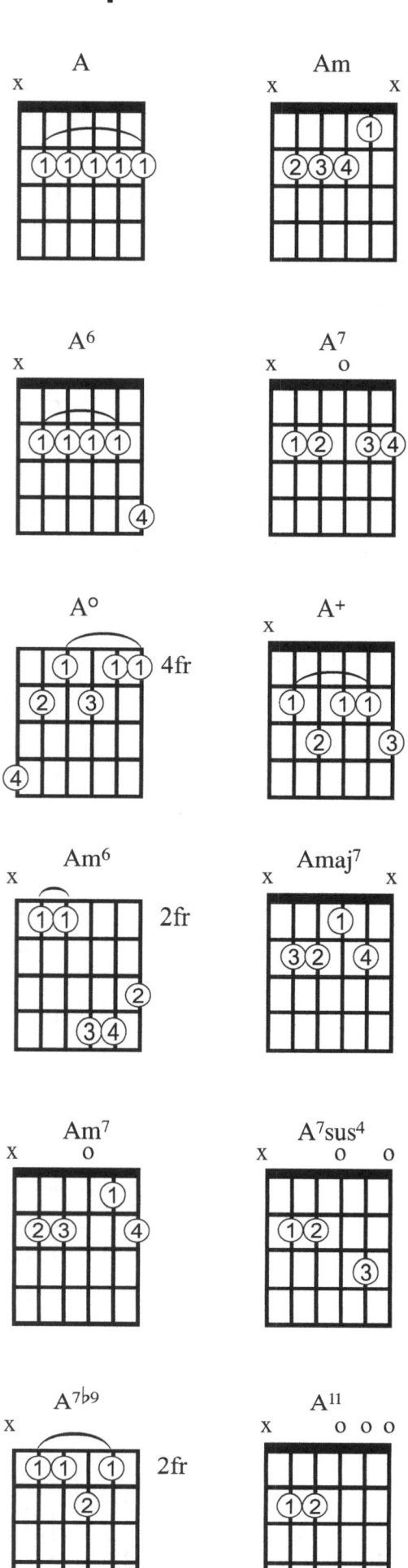

Open G: root B♭

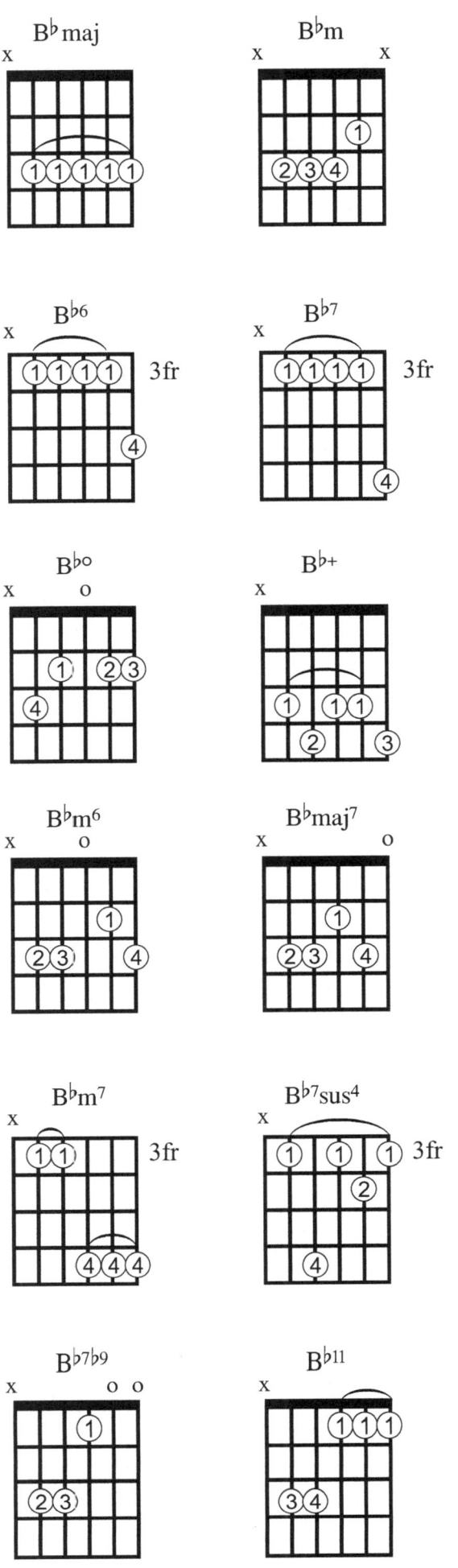

Open G: root B

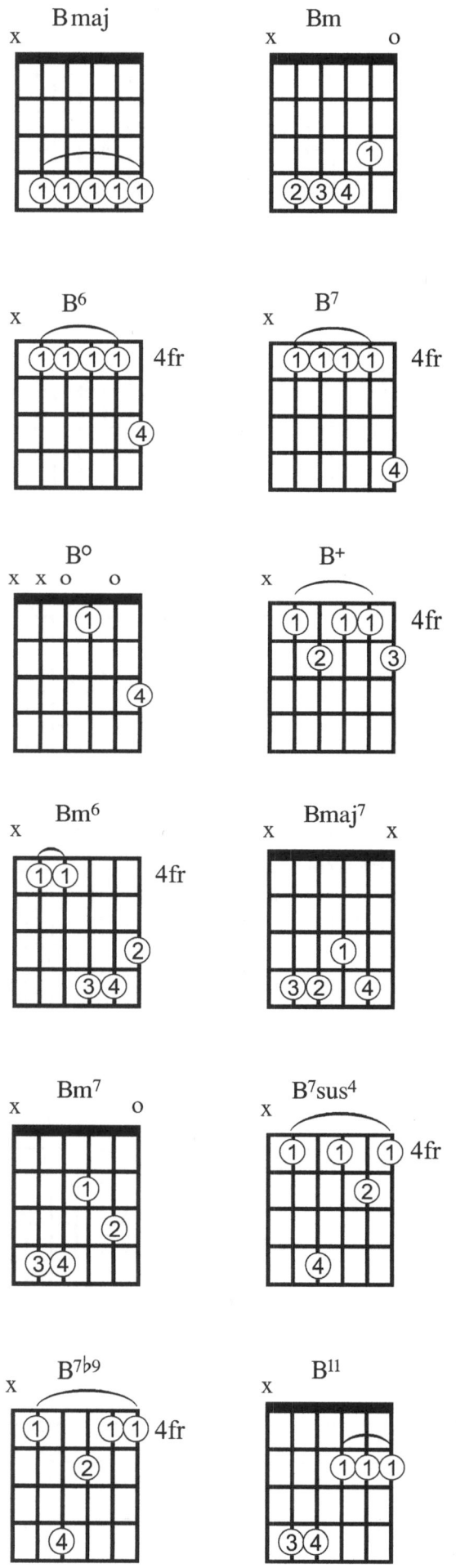

Open G: root C

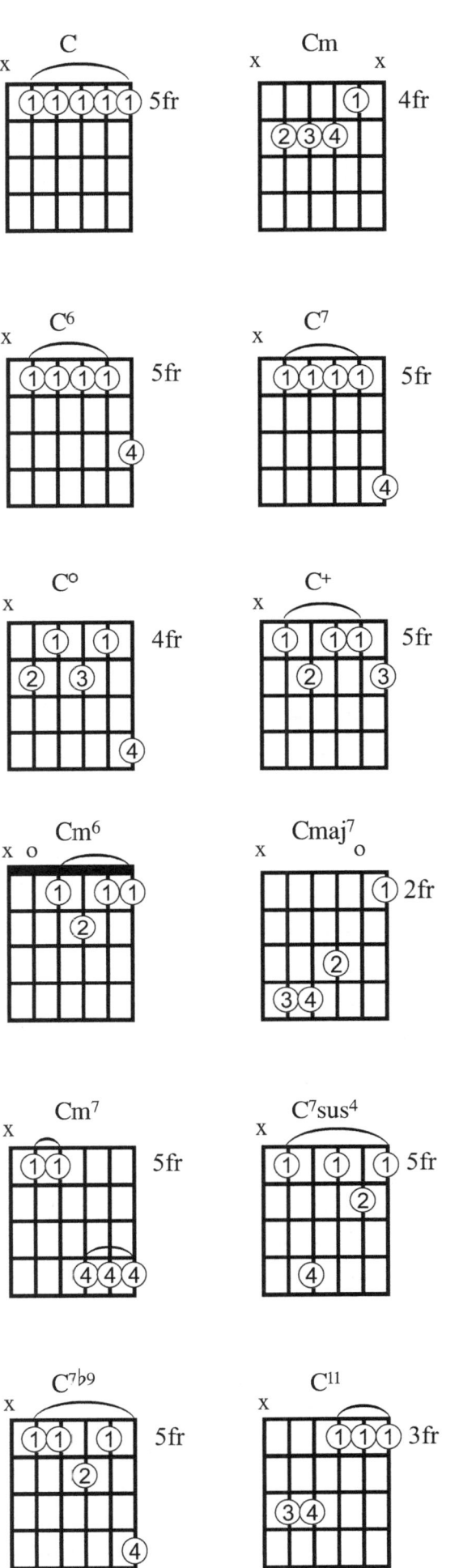

Open G: root C#

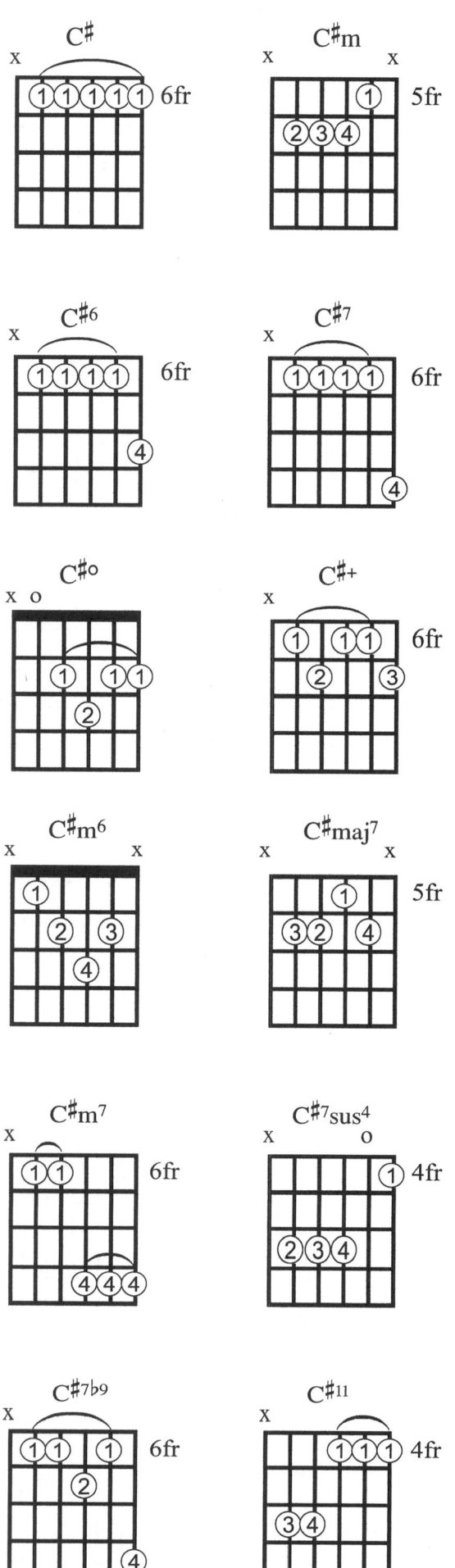

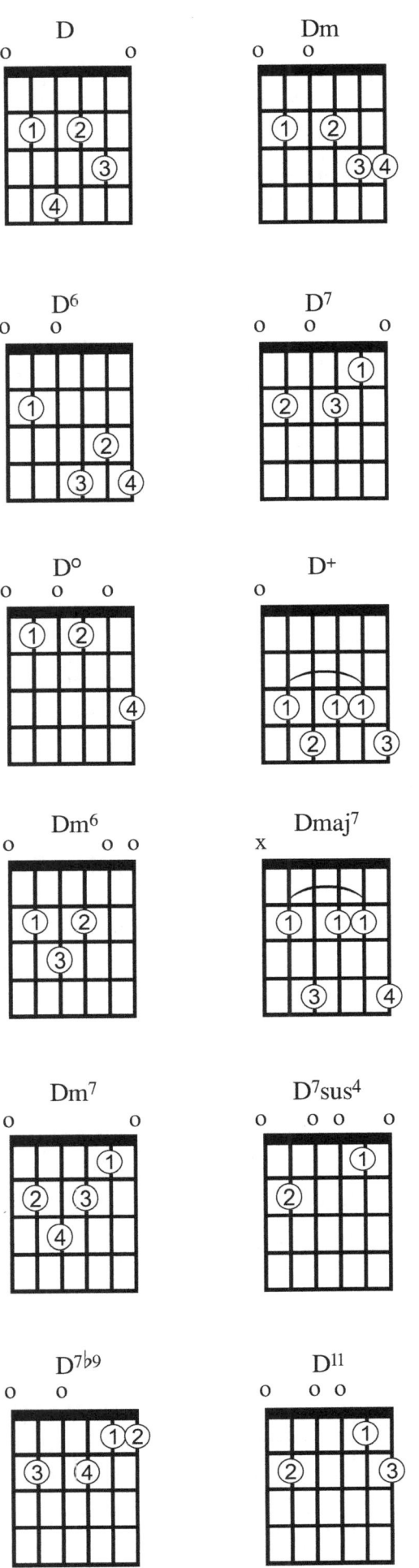

Open G: root E♭

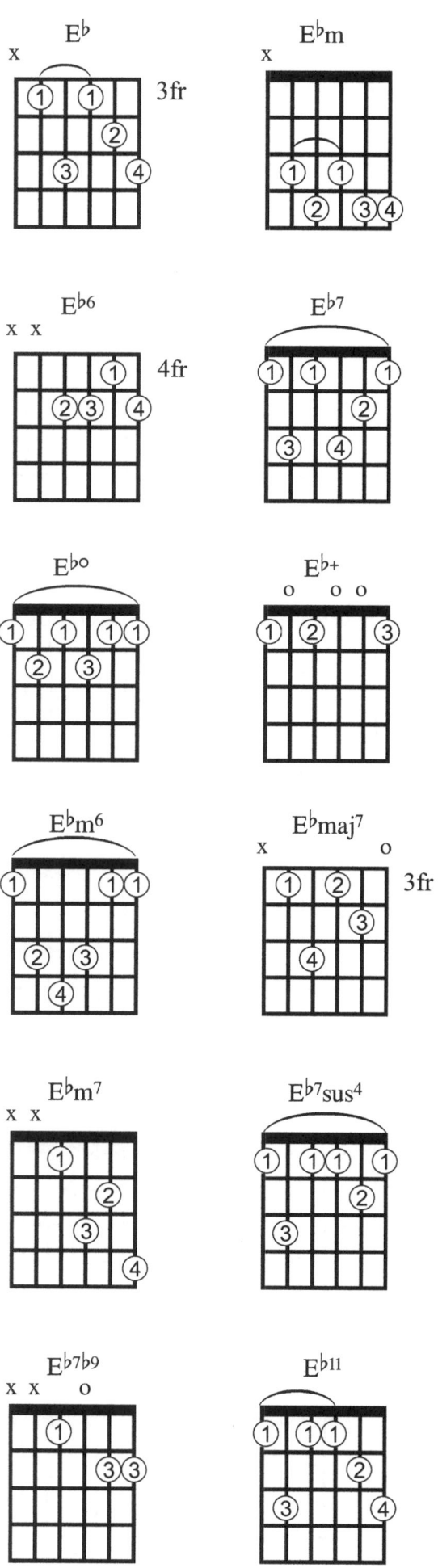

Open G: root E

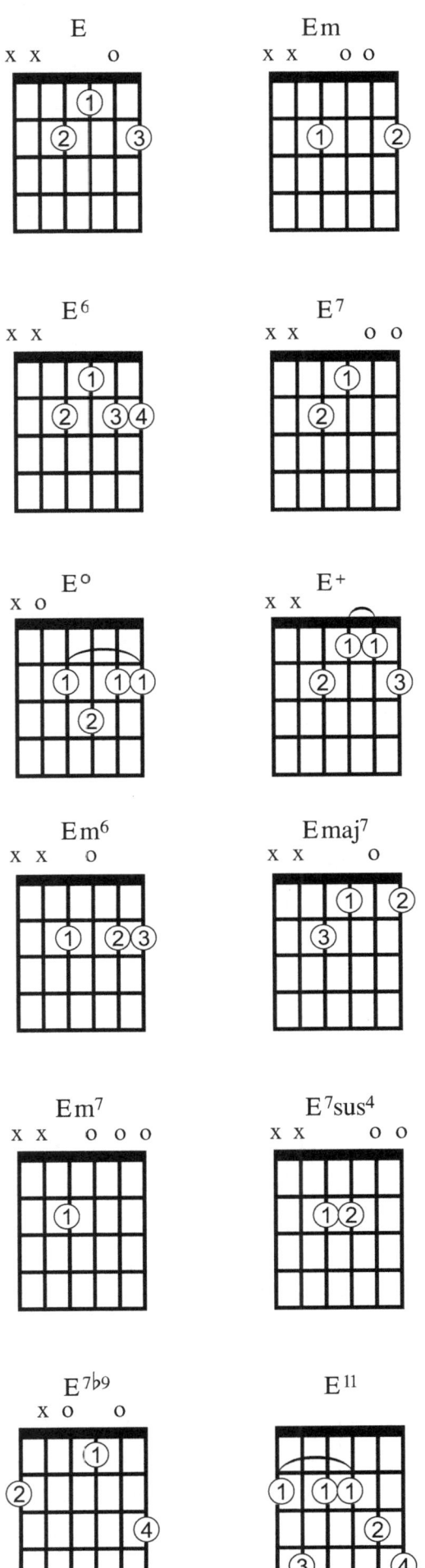

Open G: root F

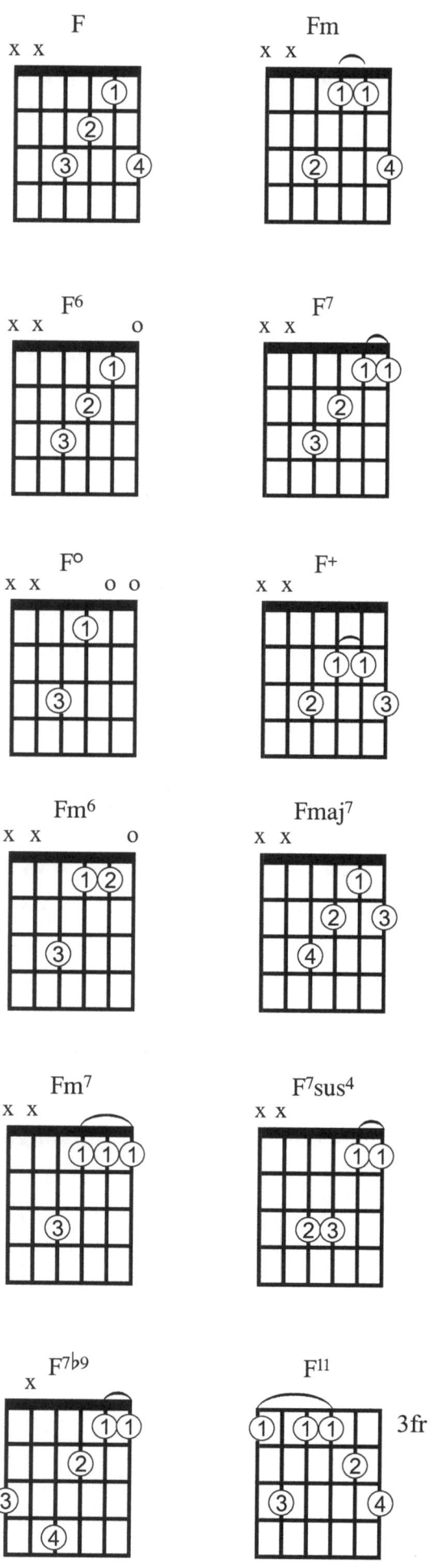

Open G: root F#

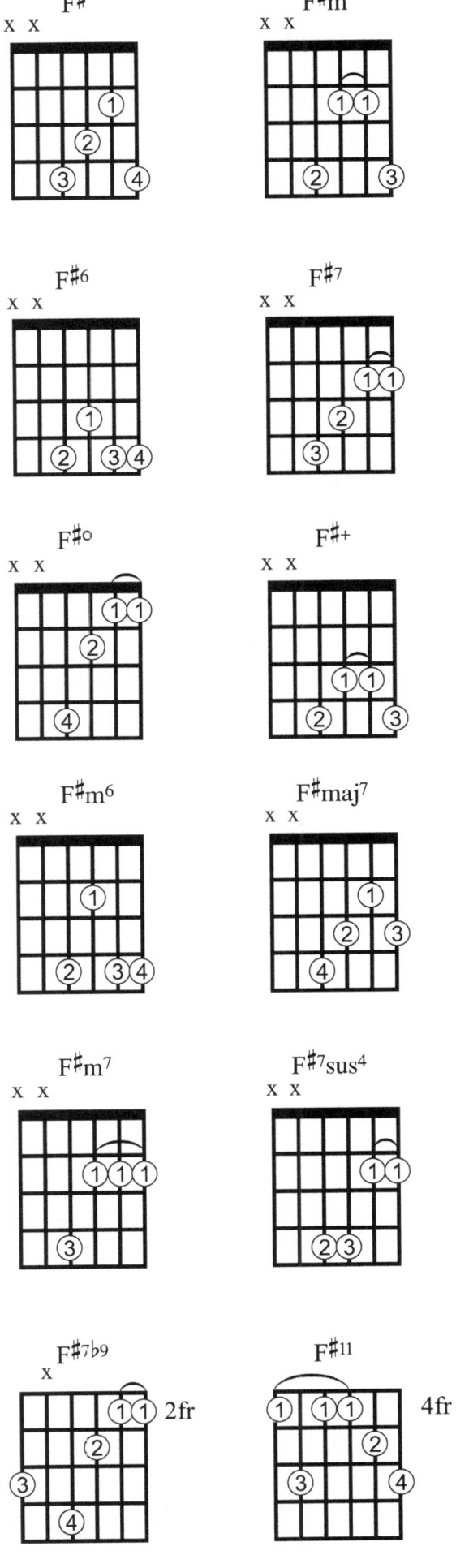

Favourite Open G Chords

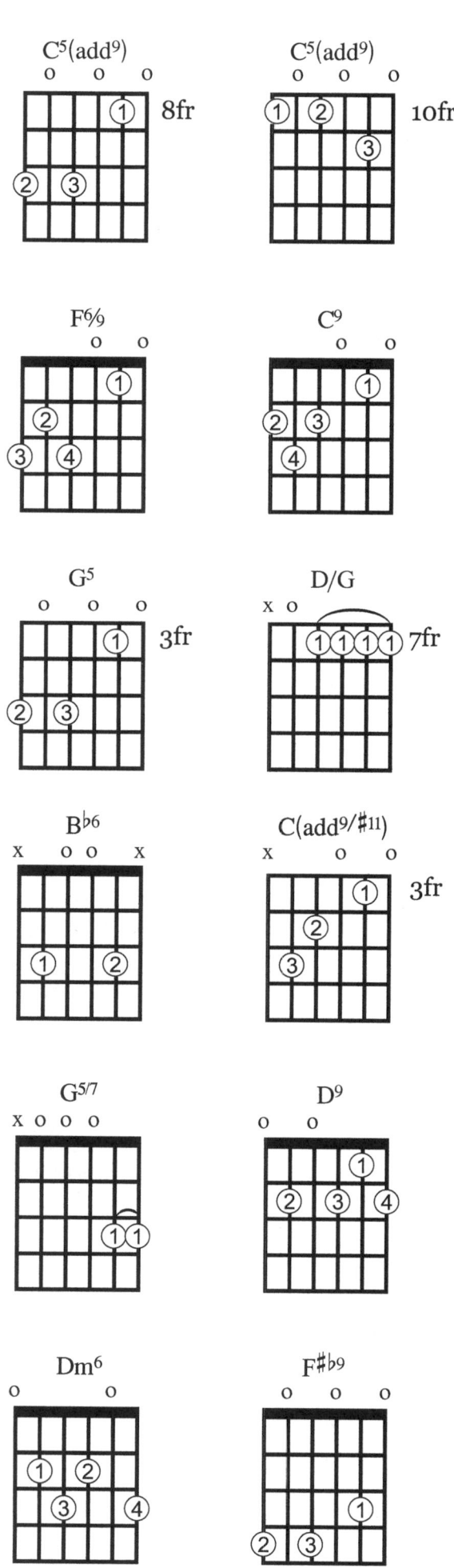

House Of The Rising Sun: Open D

My mother was a tailor, she sewed my new blue jeans
My father was a gambling man, down in New Orleans.

Now the only thing a gambler needs is a suitcase and a trunk
And the only time he's satisfied, is when he's on a drunk.

He fills his glass up to the brim, and he'll pass the cards around
And the only pleasure he gets outta life, is ramblin' from town to town.

Go tell my baby sister, not to do what I have done
But to shun that house in New Orleans they call the Rising Sun.

Well it's one foot on the platform and the other foot on the train
I'm goin' back to New Orleans to wear that ball and chain.

Well I'm goin' back to New Orleans, my race is almost run
I'm goin' back to end my life, down in the Rising Sun.

House Of The Rising Sun:
Open G

My mother was a tailor, she sewed my new blue jeans
My father was a gambling man, down in New Orleans.

Now the only thing a gambler needs is a suitcase and a trunk
And the only time he's satisfied, is when he's on a drunk.

He fills his glass up to the brim, and he'll pass the cards around
And the only pleasure he gets outta life, is ramblin' from town to town.

Go tell my baby sister, not to do what I have done
But to shun that house in New Orleans they call the Rising Sun.

Well it's one foot on the platform and the other foot on the train
I'm goin' back to New Orleans to wear that ball and chain.

Well I'm goin' back to New Orleans, my race is almost run
I'm goin' back to end my life, down in the Rising Sun.

In The Pines: Open D

My girl, my girl____ don't lie to
me tell me where did you sleep last night?
in the pines, in the pines where the sun nev-er
shines I was shiv - 'ring the whole night through.

My girl, my girl where will you go?
I'm going where the cold wind blows.
In the pines, in the pines, where the sun never shines,
I was shivering the whole night through.

My girl, my girl don't lie to me,
Tell me where did you sleep last night?
In the pines, in the pines, where the sun never shines,
I was shivering the whole night through.

My husband was a hard-working man,
Killed a mile and a half from here.
His head was found in a driving wheel,
And his body hasn't ever been found.

My girl, my girl where will you go?
I'm going where the cold wind blows.
You caused me to weep and you caused me to moan,
You caused me to leave my home.

In The Pines: Open G

My girl, my girl_____ don't lie to
me tell me where did you sleep last night?
in the pines, in the pines where the sun nev-er
shines I was shiv - 'ring the whole night through.

My girl, my girl where will you go?
I'm going where the cold wind blows.
In the pines, in the pines, where the sun never shines,
I was shivering the whole night through.

My girl, my girl don't lie to me,
Tell me where did you sleep last night?
In the pines, in the pines,where the sun never shines,
I was shivering the whole night through.

My husband was a hard-working man,
Killed a mile and a half from here.
His head was found in a driving wheel,
And his body hasn't ever been found.

My girl, my girl where will you go?
I'm going where the cold wind blows.
You caused me to weep and you caused me to moan,
You caused me to leave my home.

The Midnight Special:
Open D

Well you wake up in the morn - in'

you hear the work bell ring

and they march you to the ta - ble,

to see the same old thing.

Ain't no food up - on the ta - ble,

and no pork up in the pan.

But you bet - ter not com - plain boy,

you get in trou - ble with the man.

Chorus:

Let the mid-night spe - cial

shine a light on___ me.___

Let the mid-night spe - cial

shine a light on me.___

Let the mid - night___ spe - cial

shine a light on___ me.___

Let the mid -night spe - cial

shine a ev - er- lov- in' light on___ me.___

Yonder come Miss Rosie, how in the world did you know?
By the way she wears her apron, and the clothes she wore.
Umbrella on her shoulder, piece of paper in her hand;
She come to see the gov'nor, she wants to free her man.
Chorus

If you're ever in Houston, well, you better do the right;
You better not gamble, there, you better not fight, at all.
Or the sheriff will grab ya and the boys will bring you down.
The next thing you know, boy, oh! you're prison-bound.
Chorus

43

The Midnight Special:
Open G

Well you wake up in the morn - in'

you hear the work bell ring

and they march you to the ta - ble,

to see the same old thing.

Ain't no food up - on the ta - ble,

and no pork up in the pan.

But you bet - ter not com - plain boy,

you get in trou - ble with the man.

Yonder come Miss Rosie, how in the world did you know?
By the way she wears her apron, and the clothes she wore.
Umbrella on her shoulder, piece of paper in her hand;
She come to see the gov'nor, she wants to free her man.
Chorus

If you're ever in Houston, well, you better do the right;
You better not gamble, there, you better not fight, at all.
Or the sheriff will grab ya and the boys will bring you down.
The next thing you know, boy, oh! you're prison-bound.
Chorus

45

St. James Infirmary Blues: Open D

I went down to St. James In-firm-'ry, saw my ba - by there. She was stretched out on a long, white tab - le, so cold, so sweet, so fair. Let her go, let her go, God bless her wher-ev - er she may be, she can look this wide world ov - er, but she'll nev - er find a sweet man like me.

When I die, bury me in my straight-lace shoes.
I want a box-back coat and a Stetson hat.
Put a twenty dollar gold piece on my watch chain,
So the boys will know I died standing pat.

Give me six crap-shooting pall bearers,
Let a chorus girl sing me a song.
Put a red-hot jazz band at the top of my head,
So we can raise Hallelujah as we go along.

Folks, now that you have heard my story,
Say, boy, hand me another shot of that booze.
If anyone should ever ask you,
Tell 'em I've got those St. James Infirmary blues.

St. James Infirmary Blues: Open G

I went down_ to St. James In - firm'ry,_____

saw my ba - by there._ She was

stretched out_ on a long, white tab - le, so

cold, so sweet, so fair. Let her go,_ let her go, God

bless her wher- ev - er she may be, she can

look this wide world ov - er, but she'll

nev - er_ find a sweet man like me.

When I die, bury me in my straight-lace shoes.
I want a box-back coat and a Stetson hat.
Put a twenty dollar gold piece on my watch chain,
So the boys will know I died standing pat.

Give me six crap-shooting pall bearers,
Let a chorus girl sing me a song.
Put a red-hot jazz band at the top of my head,
So we can raise Hallelujah as we go along.

Folks, now that you have heard my story,
Say, boy, hand me another shot of that booze.
If anyone should ever ask you,
Tell 'em I've got those St. James Infirmary blues.

Recommended Listening

The following artists and albums are worth investigating for examples of open tuning:

Ry Cooder: *Paris, Texas* film soundtrack, *Paradise and Lunch*, *A Meeting By A River* (with V.M. Bhatt), *Buena Vista Social Club* with Compay Segundo et al (Ry takes a back seat but it sounds so good). This is a good cross-section of Ry's playing, finger style and slide in both Vastopol and Spanish tuning.

Robert Johnson: *The Complete Recordings* covers most of Johnson's recorded work, playing in both open tunings but tuned up a whole step to E and A respectively.

Keith Richards (with the Rolling Stones): *Exile On Main Street*, *Sticky Fingers*, *Beggars Banquet* and more are great examples of open tuned rhythm work, mostly in G, with lots of fine slide interplay from Mick Taylor.

Beck: on all of his albums there is at least one song with a big, fat, low-tuned acoustic guitar lurking in the rhythm track. Good listening for a latter-day take on open tune.

Jimmy Page (With Led Zeppelin): tracks such as *Dancing Days, Going To California* and *When The Levee Breaks* demonstrate Page's mastery of open tunings in a variety of styles.

Hawaiian Slack Key Guitar Masters: a collection on Dancing Cat Records (through Windham Hill) features the cream of Hawaii's best players, old and new, in a variety of tunings, some down as far as a low B .

Karma County: *Last Stop Heavenly Heights, Olana, Into The Land Of Promise, Happy Birthday Dear Customer, Pacifico* and **Jimmy Little's** *Messenger* and *Life's What You Make it* feature the author in mostly open D, playing finger style and slide.

Also keep an ear out for the following artists : Los Lobos, Leo Kotke, Elmore James, Joni Mitchell, Blind Willie McTell, Gabbi Pahanui, Cruel Sea, Raymond Kane, Jeff Lang, David Linley, Sol Hoopie, Shane O'Mara and G Love and Special Sauce.

1 2 3 4 5 6 7 8 9